GOSPEL REFLECTIONS

FOR SUNDAYS OF YEAR B: MARK

First Published by Messenger Publications 2017

*The right of Donal Neary SJ to be identified as the author of the Work has been asserted
by him in accordance with the Copyright and Related Rights Act, 2000.*

ISBN 978 1 910248 73 7

Designed by Messenger Publications Design Department
Printed in Ireland by Johnswood Press Limited

Messenger Publications,
37 Lower Leeson Street, Dublin D02 W938
www.messenger.ie

GOSPEL REFLECTIONS

FOR SUNDAYS OF YEAR B: MARK

DONAL NEARY SJ

The author is grateful to Logos Press, in whose missalette
these reflections were originally published
(Logos Missalette, Greystones, Co. Wicklow).

CONTENTS

Other books by the author include,
More Masses with Young People (The Columba Press)
Who Do You Say That I am? (Veritas)
Gospel Reflections for Sundays of Year C: Luke
(Messenger Publications),
Gospel Reflections for Sundays of Year A: Matthew
(Messenger Publications),
and many books of prayer for the seasons of the church year.

He frequently writes for *The Sacred Heart Messenger*,
of which he is editor.

INTRODUCTION

There's always something new in the gospel! Like going to a favourite place, climbing a mountain, meeting a friend – these are always new. Jesus speaks often of the newness of his message. He is the 'new wine'; the words of the gospel are the wineskins. In these Sunday reflections I have tried to find connecting threads between the gospel story, faith and ordinary life. It expands on consistent themes of St Ignatius of Loyola, finding God in all things, or searching for God in all things. Since ordinary life is new each day, the gospel will shine a new light on our lives.

We are pilgrims listening to the gospel on different levels: the words of Jesus reach the heart. This book is not an exegesis or scriptural commentary on the gospel, or a link between all the readings, useful as these are, but rather the book is intended to encourage you to follow Jesus, the 'way, truth and life'; my hope is that these reflections will appeal at different times to your mind, heart and hopes.

The reflections can also help you in the preparation of a theme for Sundays in a liturgy group, or to prepare to hear the gospel reading or reflect on it during the week.

We may sometimes become aware of a new aspect to a story. This can be achieved in reading the reflections alone or together, sharing in a group, or reading books that explicate and contextualise the gospels.

Each page gives the gospel reference; nothing can replace reading the gospel text, and the reflections bring them to life for us, especially as we can become accustomed to them with hearing them so often.

Above all, may they bring us closer to the Lord Jesus who wants to come close to us in his word, and his word is a human, warm, loving word, rooted in our lives and in his preaching and mission.

Donal Neary SJ

1ˢᵀ SUNDAY OF ADVENT

The Invitation

I like these words of the late Cardinal Hume: 'There are times when I can visualise Our Lord at the break of day standing by my bed and saying: "Get up, follow me". Whether I am conscious of it or not, in effect that invitation, that loving but insistent command, is given to me every day. Each new morning is the opportunity to start again. Yesterday there may have been inadequacies and failures but today Christ renews his call: "Follow me. I have chosen you. I need you". Who can fail to respond to the thought that God needs our willing collaboration.'

We are carers of creation and of his people. Take this seriously, it is our world. God has made himself so vulnerable and this gospel reading is just before the passion. An area or parish improves if enough people do something. We look at areas in a locality which are now clean of drugs, more prosperous and just. This has been due to the work of people co-creating the world with God. Making it a better place. Doing the world a world of good.

The gospel today says, don't give up, God is always near! Live in hope and preparation. Stay awake to the season – the ways we can deepen and grow in our faith – maybe do a retreat, do something good for others with your time or finance, notice God in the events of the next few weeks, pray a bit every day, make time to be awakened to the centre of our world who is God, and to his central action in creating the world each day, sending Jesus Christ his Son.

A question for the first week of Advent:
how can I help someone today?
Lord, send me, use me, create me for your work in the world.

2ND SUNDAY OF ADVENT

Weeks of Mercy

There's a family expectancy in the air about Christmas, people are looking forward to the celebration. Even if we dread bits of Christmas, and many do, we know that there is something very good about it. We look forward to it, as we look forward to the visit of someone we love, a holiday or a break from work.

The people in Jesus' time were like that – they looked forward to the 'one who is to come'. It would all take time, and the last of the messengers was John the Baptist. His mother awaited his birth with huge expectation.

He preached forgiveness. This is one of the special gifts of God, and one of the big celebrations of Advent. We are a forgiven people, and we welcome the forgiveness of God in our repentance. This means, first, that we are grateful for forgiveness, that we do not have to carry forever the burden of sin, meanness or our faults and failings. God covers them over in mercy. Second, we welcome forgiveness to try to do better in life – to move on from sinfulness and meanness to a life of care, compassion, love and joy. It is a call and a challenge to forgive others.

Advent is not complete without some admission of sin and our need for mercy. The parish celebrations of the sacrament of Penance (Reconciliation) in common, or individually, is a step which makes our celebration of Christmas complete.

For this week: say the angelus upon waking, at noon and at 6 p.m.
May our good and gracious God have mercy on us all, forgive us our
sins and lead us to everlasting life. Amen.

1:1–18

3ʳᵈ SUNDAY OF ADVENT

The Joy of Waiting

Advent is a time of joy, the joy of waiting. This Sunday, we wear the joyful rose-coloured vestment. The messenger in the first reading is the 'joyful messenger', and his joy is that God is near and God is coming. This would be the message of Jesus – that he was the joyful messenger of his Father's love. He would be the shepherd – the one who cares, knows and actively looks after the sheep. John the Baptist is the voice of joy and energy, preaching the new message.

Voices of Advent bring God near – the central message within all the voices of Christmas. God's Christmas voice is *I love you, you are all brothers and sisters, and nothing except love is final.*

This is not just a voice ... but it is actively loving in word and deed. One way of touching that love is the Mass. Jesus is not really love from the sky, but food of the Eucharist, that nourishes us and makes a difference. We bring our ordinary concerns to Mass, and let God lighten them and transform them, and enlighten us with his word. The voice of God makes sense of, and brings light into, the ordinariness of life.

God is present in his word, and in his body – we wait in joy for the Word to be made flesh.

Remember this week what makes you joyful about the coming feast of Christmas and be grateful.
Lord I believe your word was made flesh and appeared among us.

LUKE 1:26–38

4ᵀᴴ SUNDAY OF ADVENT

Annunciations Big and Small

I got stuck miles away in a small village and had no access to public transport. It was a public holiday, so I had to stay put. A family were kind enough to put me up for the night and feed me! This was an annunciation for me! Annunciations announce the coming of the Lord, favour from God. Life is full of little and big annunciations. Ways in which we bring the Son of God alive within the world. The beginning now of what would later be the resurrection event.

For Mary it was in the ordinary – maybe at the well, as she collected the water for the day. Or in her house. Any time we find genuine help, compassion, justice – all the gifts of God's Spirit – it is an annunciation. It can be an annunciation of new faith and love in God. What Mary got at annunciation was the overshadowing of the Holy Spirit and the Son of God in her womb.

We are the people who find grace and hope in the middle of everything; maybe in a busy shop, the middle of a bus journey, with the children, friends and family, at Mass or prayer. It can happen anywhere.

There is always a response. If we have been gifted, we give. Someone let me out of the carpark and I let the next person out. Someone visited me in hospital and I did the same later. Our Christmas way of celebration and helping others is a response to annunciation.

Let the big mystery of God's love get deeply into you at this time of year.

Remember when you felt close to God's presence
in your life and give thanks.
Welcome, Lord Jesus.

CHRISTMAS DAY

God's Door

Most cribs have an open door. This is God's door: it is never closed to us. An important message to us today is welcoming and openness. The bonds of Christmas are strong; of memories, love, faith, grief and hope. We remember that with each other we meet and we share life – we grow together.

Bonds can be strong or limited. The bond with a cousin to whom we send a card is not as active a bond as the family we meet regularly and help, support and love. We meet at funerals and weddings. Better that, however, than never meeting at all. Bonds can renew love, even if there are blocks to our relationship. Bonds are made up of love and quarrels, attractions and histories, of all sorts of good and bad things. Even the person who does not go home for Christmas thinks of home these days. Our Christian faith may be a bond. Christmas faith may be a bit like 'we only meet at Christmas'! Isn't it good we meet at Christmas and strengthen these bonds among us? Bonds of love, family, neighbourhood and faith. Something of God and the community of the Church, binds us this time of year.

We are invited this night to find the real Christmas again and that the message lasts through the year. We find that God is close and near, and that his word involves us with others – especially with the poor and the migrant, the sinner and the saint. All are called together in him. We visit the poor infant born on the side of the road to make us remember at other times that many are born like that today, that many are poor, and many need the drastic help which Mary and Joseph needed that night.

Give thanks for the good Christmases and ask help for any painful memories to place in the crib. O come let us adore him.

FEAST OF THE HOLY FAMILY

God is Not Fussy!

In the gospels, Jesus' family life is hardly described. Like all of us, his family would have had a big influence on his life. Because of its importance, the Church has always placed a great value on the family.

The reality these days is that family life is now very varied: divorced and separated parents, gay parents, widowed parents; while caring for all, the Church proposes the family of the mother and father, where possible, as the ideal.

We commit ourselves as a church to finding solutions to homelessness and poverty affecting families. We need to be aware of the stresses of family life, to understand them and find funding for caring for them, especially children.

No matter what, there are stresses in family life – the sacrament of marriage promises the help of God and the community.

The Church encourages family prayer, like visiting the crib with children at Christmas, and making the most of religious occasions in the family. The gospel today is about the life of Jesus growing in humanity and wisdom. He was brought to the temple; Mary and Joseph taught him to pray.

There is a special presence of God in the family: God is present in close love – in all the aspects of family life.

God isn't very fussy about where He lives, moves and has his being – sometimes it's even in a wonderfully imperfect family!

May the prayers of Mary and Joseph help us in our family life.
Bless us, O Lord, with the joy of love,
and strengthen all families in your loving care.

2ND SUNDAY AFTER CHRISTMAS

Season of Light

We are in a season of lights – candle lights, Christmas lights, lights on the street and hanging on the houses. Let the season ask us: what light enlightens our lives? What light do we live by?

Jesus is presented as an image of the true light. His gospel shines light into our lives, and lets our light shine.

We live by the light of Jesus by listening to his word, living by his example and in prayer. Pope Francis recommends, 'Today, for example, try for ten minutes – fifteen, no more – to read the gospel, picture what happens, and say something to Jesus. And nothing more. And so your knowledge of Jesus will be bigger and your hope will grow. Do not forget, keeping our eyes fixed on Jesus.'

We allow his light shine within us by watching him in the gospel. The word of God is not just a series of human words, but a person who is the Son of God. We find this light in prayer.

Later in his ministry, Jesus will speak of letting our light shine. The light within us from God is not just for ourselves but to be shared for others.

That is the light of Christmas, if we can shine this light for a few days, why not for the rest of the year?

On the inbreath, imagine the light of God filling your body;
on the outbreath, send that light to another.
Let your light, O Lord, shine within me,
and let it brighten the lives of those around me.

BAPTISM OF OUR LORD

New Energy

Jesus' baptism by John was a special moment. The real coming of God's spirit upon him, the Spirit who had come on Mary at the moment of Jesus' conception, and would be with Jesus at his last moments on the Cross.

The spirit brings him new energy. This feast marks that something new is happening, and that Jesus knows he is the beloved son; from eternity and into time.

The Spirit came upon him – but not just for himself. He would send the Spirit later to us, to help us to forgive and to persevere in doing good.

This is a feast about energy. Jesus found a new spirit in himself after his prayer and he heard words he would never forget. Maybe you have heard words of love from someone you will never forget. They give energy to the heart and soul, inspiring us to be always on the go, ready for new life within us.

The Spirit pours the energy of God into bread and wine and they are changed forever. He sends himself forever, sending the love and presence and energy of God.

We know that we can get stuck. We need new infusions of the Spirit to renew our energy. Can we be the type of people who others think it's good to meet? Can we be people open to the Spirit of God, open to new life, new love and fully being the individuals we can be?

Recall your baptism: imagine water being poured over you,
and allow this love of God to fill you today.
Lord, thank you for the gift of Baptism.

1ST SUNDAY OF LENT

What my Lent does for Others

Every Lent is a new beginning; sometimes beginnings are welcomed, other times it's a case of half and half! We welcome Lent as a time to make our faith fresh, but we know from other Lents that it's hard to keep going, and it lasts a long time! We might wonder about the true purpose of Lent.

The focus of Lent is not on what we give up but on what we are given. We focus our minds on the self-giving love of Jesus which we will celebrate in Holy Week. We allow ourselves to believe in this love. Often it's difficult to believe in the tender love of God, but it conquers all else in the world; it is given in the mercy and compassion of God.

Lent pours the grace of forgiveness into our world, which we need individually and as a people. We need to know that God is bigger than any of our sins, wars, violence and hatred. God wants his kingdom to come now. Lent is our time of saying 'yes' to a partnership with God in saving the world from the effects of evil and sin.

Maybe we can ask what our Lent does for others, rather than just what we are doing for Lent. It is a time of renewal, which shows in love, forgiveness and care of others in our lives.

Pray a little, read the gospel every day, do something good for another every day – these are the ways to share in the saving love of God.
Lord, by your cross and resurrection you have set us free;
you are the saviour of the world.

2ND SUNDAY OF LENT

Radiant Light

Jesus heard at the Transfiguration that he was beloved! We all want to know that someone would say that they love us.

We are God's favoured ones. We live in the big wide world of God's love, and Jesus on Tabor was allowing himself to be loved in the radiant light of God, shining even in the cloud.

Together we are loved as Peter, James and John were loved in community. Light is caught from one to the other. We are the light of Tabor Mountain for each other – all are loved. Those whom I like and those I like less! The radiant body of Christ was hammered and killed later by ourselves. Love killed at Calvary rose again. Love cannot die.

We can transfigure or disfigure each other. We can bring out the light and the hope and the joy in our belonging to God!

We can transfigure a school, a parish, a community or any group by first of all our being loved by God and letting love emit from ourselves. If we really believe we are loved by God, then the world we live in is transfigured – changed utterly.

In the light of the cross, the sign of our faith, the way, we are saved.

Imagine yourself breathing in the light of God.
Let it fill your body bit by bit. Praise God for this light.
Light of God, love me, save me, call me.

3RD SUNDAY OF LENT

God's Building

Why is Jesus angry? They have missed the point and the religious leaders are allowing this to happen! Religion has come down to ritual, and the centre is missing. Jesus was not much at home in the temple. He went there sometimes, and always caused trouble. The finding in the temple, the words – my body is the temple. Jesus is more at home at the table – the loaves at the lake, the fish on the beach, the last supper in a home. This is where he is most himself.

The falsity of the occasion was the use of the temple to entrap by riches. The poor were being overcharged to pay for the materials for sacrifices. This caused the anger of Jesus.

The temple has disappeared. We are God's building. If we do not make God's presence real in our area, then maybe we should knock down the church! Only if God is alive in us all the time, will he be alive in the building. If God is not alive all week in us, God will not be alive on Sunday. If he is not alive in our hearts – well, maybe that's sometimes why religion can be so boring – it's religion only from the neck up.

The forty-six years are now over, and the three days of the rebuilding have been going on for years in the hearts of all who are faithful to God's love. The building continues still and we are the living stones.

Think of what is most central to your life.
Is that a concern of God too?
Lord, keep me close to all you love and value in life.

JOHN 3:14–21

4ᵀᴴ SUNDAY OF LENT

A New Colour

Why rose vestments today? It represents the hope of Easter just around the corner. We are on the way, but not there yet. So we wear the colours of joy. Our joy is from the love which has brought us here and made us the work of art that we are. Jesus is lifted up on the cross so that we may have life. In all our thoughts on lent and the death of Jesus, we are people of the resurrection.

We have many identities in our lives, but our prime belonging is to God as brothers and sisters of Jesus. This is the life of faith, the life of faith in the heart.

We can often think of God and faith as deadening. Our faith is that he sent his son from love. Jesus is the one who went through all we go through and then rose from death. As our faith in this becomes strong, then we find God's active love in our lives. At times, when there is little else there, we unite ourselves with the sufferings of Jesus and rise with him. God, being love, promises not an easy life nor magical solutions, but love always.

We live on amazing grace, and the graced light is Christ. Easter is around the corner, if we take a corner too quickly we crash. In life there is often a call to be patient. We live in the light of Easter.

Look on the world – its business, goodness and evil,
and let God's love for the world become your love.
Lord, by your cross and resurrection, you have set us free;
you are the saviour of the world.

5TH SUNDAY OF LENT

Approaches to Suffering

I knew a man who fought cancer to the end. He took to every type of possible healing. We had all been told it wouldn't work. I know another who just opened himself to it all and wouldn't even take chemo. These are different approaches to suffering. One fought it and the other accepted. I admired the both of them.

Many people go into hospital wondering about their illness, and worry that death might be close. That's part of life. As for Jesus: it's a fearful time, confusing and sometimes draws us into more faith. We can transform our pain into suffering, and find some great graces in it. There is the challenge to find new life in it. Pain becomes suffering. Jesus doesn't want the chalice of the garden, but he allows it become fully part of him so that his inner strength is big! It doesn't mean a simplistic approach, rather it means an acceptance of darkness in life.

Jesus found in his passion that God the Father is near. This can be our way and we can find that through helping each other. We can help people at times of suffering – listening, being present. We find this in our hearts, not in books – we find that we can grow through suffering and we realise on a bad day that peace invades the soul, or that there is a bright light in the darkness.

In any suffering in our lives, when we think of God, or say his name,
or question him, maybe we can just imagine a light around us.
Saying nothing, just being open to the light.
Lord, by your cross and resurrection, you have set us free;
you are the saviour of the world.

PALM SUNDAY

Two Parades

There are two parades of Holy week. First, into Jerusalem from Bethany on the Sunday and Jesus being acclaimed as a political saviour. People hoped he would triumph, that his followers would put him into power, and all hoped that he would get rid of the Romans.

The second, from Jerusalem, outside the walls of the city on the following Friday, to Calvary; a man in disgrace. A man carrying his cross, crowned with thorns, mocked, bullied and tortured. About to be killed. Like the parade to a dishonoured graveside.

He had all sorts of followers – some like camp followers, some terrorists, some people on the make for themselves, or the ones who stayed until the end, like his mother, an aunt and a few of the followers. The others were at a distance, they would come back, and would follow later to the end.

We hope to be in that second parade.

Palms are for waving in triumph, then they wither. The cross is forever, for all time.

The cross is his love, and as we follow in this parade we show our willingness to console him in love to the end.

This is a holy week because a man like us, and one of the Trinity, gave his life.

Look at a crucifix and say, 'What will I do for Christ?'
Lord, by your cross and resurrection, you have set us free;
you are the saviour of the world.

EASTER SUNDAY

Our Celebration

If we have a look around the church we notice colour, nature, icons, water and oil. We hear joyful music and uplifting prayer. This is for Easter – our celebration.

The next bit of Easter is to go and tell. Like he appeared in an ordinary garden, he appeared to the unexpected ones, the women. Who would have thought he'd do that? He would still do the same!

The divine Jesus also looks ordinary. They take a while to recognise that it's the same Jesus, the one they knew and loved. We sometimes meet people who got a promotion (or something else big happened for them) and we realise that deep down they are still the same person. Jesus was new but then they realised that for now and forever he would still be the same, finding us and loving us in the ordinary, on our good days and bad days, in goodness and weakness.

On our bad days he can bring the best out of us. Like his bad days brought out the best in him. When we can say little, he sings *Alleluia* in us. He is doing us a world of good so we could do the world a world of good.

His words of resurrection echo today in all that is in this church, its colour, sounds, and above all in the humanity here. We will always have the echo of Jesus, he is risen today: alleluia, alleluia.

Allow the joy of Jesus to fill your heart as your breath fills your body.
Risen Lord, be joyful in me, in all.

JOHN 20:19–31

2ND SUNDAY OF EASTER

Growing in Faith

Our Church community faces many big questions about the place of women, our views on sexuality, the need for consultation and for dialogue. We need to know what all of us believe, not just our leaders. We need to know how people find it to live their faith in the areas of sexuality, justice, migration, ministry and other realities today. Recent synods and letters of the Pope have tried to connect theory and lived faith.

There is a need to be able to grapple with the demands of today and the message of the gospel; to be able to discern our path in the peace and joy of the Easter message, knowing that we don't all have to agree with each other to say 'my Lord and my God'.

We are the people who are happy to believe; to show we are a community of faith and of joy, and we want to spread this faith that lives for justice and compassion.

We will never get it fully right, but we can get better and better if we unite with the Lord and hear each other with respect. That is our challenge at Easter. May the Lord bring the best out of our faith in bad days, and help us live with and enjoy the best of our faith in the good times. We want to make alive what is best in our Christianity.

Thomas doubted at times;
can I share my doubts of belief with the Lord?
Lord, I believe in you, strengthen my belief.

3RD SUNDAY OF EASTER

The Sacred in the Ordinary

It is interesting that it is hard to find a painting of their late-night meal of fish. Other images crowd the online search results. The garden, the breakfast on the beach, the road to Emmaus – old and new pictures. Is the fish meal too ordinary for the resurrection? We can't believe that the Lord of all creation who died for us will be recognised so simply, or can we?

Jesus is in a bit of a fix. Faith is still weak in his followers – how can he get to them? Though the doors are closed, he comes among them in their fear. He said peace again, but this doesn't seem to get through. Finally, he tried a meal of ordinary fish with them and somehow it got through. They remembered other meals of fish and the way he ate it. Faith is growing in them in the simple act of sharing a meal together.

There is always another way for Jesus. We resist that he is so ordinary. The resurrection happens now and in the ordinary. How did I find the resurrection this week? Where I took a jump outside of the self in love, care and work for justice? In any way we raise each other up to a better human life and faith, then the resurrection is being shared.

The garden, the chat on the road and now the ordinary meal. Imagine if we said he took fish, said the blessing…! All of life is sacred, and soaked through with the love and grace of the Risen Lord.

In your breathing in and out, echo the word 'peace'.
Lord, make me a means of your peace.

4TH SUNDAY OF EASTER

Called at Baptism

Following one's vocation is a response from within to the needs outside us. A decision to work for the poor or assist people in need is not necessarily a vocation. A vocation meets the human needs of the world but with a motivation from within. We care for our children and grandchildren not just because they are sick or insecure, but because we love them. This love will move us out to help them in various situations.

We find a call to be 'people for others' because our heart teaches us that with Jesus we are all brothers and sisters, and that God wants to save the world, and needs our help to do so.

This is the Sunday we all pray that our particular vocation in life may become clear and may become stronger.

Each of us are called to love God and love our neighbour. This is the first Christian calling at our Baptism; we then find the best way for each of us with our own particular set of gifts, talents and weaknesses to live out that call to love.

We think today especially of religious life and priesthood. There are needs for priests, sisters and brothers in most parts of the world. As a community, in families and parishes, we thank those who have given their lives in these vocations and pray that they may increase.

> *Remember with thanks those whose lives*
> *have given you your faith in God.*
> *Lord, thanks for what I can do in your service.*
> *May your kingdom come!*

5ᵀᴴ SUNDAY OF EASTER

Jesus, the Centre

Without a unifying centre, groups lose their way. A sports team which sets its eyes on money, rather than on teamwork, will lose games. A family which relies on anything other than love to keep it together will fall apart. The Church, the community of Jesus, is something similar.

What keeps the Church together, and at its best, is Jesus. Human leadership, moral authority or ritual dogmatism, are not the centre(s) of the Church. Leadership can fail, moral authority can take wrong turns and ritual dogmatism can override the concerns of people. The centre of the Church is Jesus Christ. Our unity with Jesus is the central bond of the Church. He is the vine, we are the branches.

When we have been let down by the Church, like in situations of abuse, or cover-ups by Church authority, we are kept going as Christians by our unity with Jesus.

The image of roots and branches – of fruit and tree, all very much part of each other – is what Jesus uses to convey this unity.

Only if we can look on Jesus Christ as the centre of our faith can Church life be sincere and have the energy which will save and change our world.

Imagine yourself being with Jesus; just the two of you. Share what is
in your heart and listen to how his word echoes within you.
May we dwell in you, Lord, as you dwell in us.
Give us your peace, your energy, your joy.

JOHN 15:9–17

6TH SUNDAY OF EASTER

The One Commandment – Only One

This gospel is like a vision statement or a mission statement from Jesus. It is about finding joy in listening to Jesus, how to live the good life in love with one another, how to love oneself in the love of God, and in directing our lives to bear fruit that will generate love.

It is so central that it is read at many really important moments of Christian life. it is one of the most popular readings at a wedding, linking the love of God and human love at such a special time.

Jesus' love was to lay down his life in a specific way. Our love grounds our life often in many unforgotten ways. Hours spent with a sick child or parent, years caring for someone ill, leaving home on missionary assignments; giving up something for children. The message is a big challenge in simple ways for most of us.

Isn't it a joy to know that the most enjoyable mystery of life, love, is the only commandment of God? This shows us that God is on our side. His commandment is to do what we want most to do and experience – to love and be loved. Even when the love costs us something.

Recall a time when you felt you were really loving someone.
Become aware that you were then very near to God.
Thank you, Lord, for love given and received in my life.

ASCENSION

Going Out or Going Up?

The feast of the Ascension seems to be more about the apostles going out than Jesus going up! As Jesus goes to his Father, the message is for us now, and to be witnesses to him, sharing what we have received and heard.

Witnesses to a road accident often contradict one another. They misremember what they saw or heard, or they may have only glanced at the event and moved on without taking in all the available information. We can be witnesses of Jesus who stayed with the event, not just with a glance. We have seen and heard the best story ever told, and the most influential life ever lived.

We witness to Jesus in prayer, in reading the gospel and in service of others in love. Prayer means being in touch with God, who is reaching out to us. The gospel is what feeds us, a daily opening to the words and deeds of Jesus. Loving service brings us to witness the care of God, as we give and receive care.

This is what we give to the ascended Lord and receive from him. The word of God is the divine word in human diction. In our work for him, God is linking heaven and earth and we share in his divinity as he does in our humanity. Far from being the absence of Jesus, the Ascension is his presence in a new way among us.

Looking up is a religious gesture.
Look up to the skies sometimes this week and make a favourite prayer.
Lord, may your kingdom come!

PENTECOST SUNDAY

Spirit of Unity

The effect of the Holy Spirit at the first Pentecost was to create unity – the incident of people understanding different languages should not be taken literally, but rather should be read that deep divisions among people can be overcome by the Spirit of God. Many of the gifts of the Spirit – trust, love and patience – in the second reading are about a deep unity among us. These and other gifts of the Spirit bring unity at a deep level in families, friendships, all kinds of relationships and communities.

The effects of disunity can lead to violence and wars. No wonder Jesus prayed so often for unity – and his Spirit would unite us in the end.

Disagreements may happen in the healthiest of relationships, but often lead often to peace eventually. Dividedness never leads to peace and is never from God.

A Pentecost unity can be seen in the reconciliation between Jesus' natural family and the new family of the apostles. A gospel account says that in the upper room were people like James, his family 'brother' and Mary, his mother, who was the uniting love of all Jesus' followers.

On the inbreath, breathe in the Spirit of God,
the wind that blows where it will.
Come Holy Spirit;
Fill our hearts.
Bring your peace and unity
To our world.
May your kingdom come
and your will be done.
Amen.

TRINITY SUNDAY

Father, Son and Spirit

When you think of the word Spirit, do you think of something lively? I think of a sort of flowing, living water, or a cycle race, rather than a traffic jam; the flow of life in us, rather than the ways we block life. It is the spirit of God whom we call Father, Son or Christ and Spirit. We live in that sort of love. The Church is called to be that sort of community.

The Trinity can make God seem totally distant, but that is not Jesus! He is the one who gets right into life, bringing God into humanity as one of us. Jesus spoke so much about farming, weddings, death, illness, joys, trust, creation, nature, breakfasts, gardens and dinners; he is the God of the table more than the God of the temple. His spirit flows in all of creation, love, suffering and joy; he finds us in all things.

We need to have that *big* view of God. He makes everything sacred. Even the name Father, Son and Spirit.

Our call is to flow with him, to go with the flow of God's Spirit. We are the flow of God in the world. We become what we receive – the love of the Trinity in the world. We become like Christ himself as we receive this bread of life, called to be his witnesses. By what we say and do and in all we are.

Give thanks to the Lord for his presence in the Eucharist.
Father, Son and Spirit, enfold me in love, the love of your eternal life.

FEAST OF THE BODY AND BLOOD OF THE CHRIST

Gift for all Time

The main feast of the Eucharist is Holy Thursday. The Corpus Christi feast originated partly to stress the joy of the Eucharist, which might be somewhat lost in the more sombre Holy week. While Holy Thursday also includes the washing of the feet, this feast is simply to commemorate the gift of Jesus in the Eucharist.

The body and blood of Jesus is the life of the Lord 'given to us'. This gift is for all times. At scenes where Jesus feeds the people in the gospel, there is always much food left over. This is a sign of him wanting to give his love for the life of the world for all time. This life, to death and resurrection, is commemorated in a real way at every Mass.

When a priest or minister gives communion, we are aware of the special moment this is for so many people. It is a moment of asking for help in life, for peace of mind, for the presence of the Lord. At a time of illness or bereavement we may recall the lift of grace when communion was brought to us. On our side it is our promise also to share the Lord in different ways of love in our own lives.

*Remember a time when receiving Communion
brought you peace, joy or comfort.
It is right and just, O Lord, to give you thanks
for the gift of yourself in the Eucharist.*

2ND SUNDAY IN ORDINARY TIME

Good things take time

We need time for the best things in life to come to fruition. Love grows in marriage, friendship and family over many years. Love has significant moments but often it cannot be rushed. Jesus' disciples were invited to stay with him the rest of that day to get to know him; it would not happen immediately at the river. 'Rest of the day' would mean a very long time.

How well do I know Jesus? How much do I know about him? These questions represent two different types of knowledge; I can know everything about a person and not know the person.

What do I find out about Jesus in this reading? He is one who does not force himself on people, he asks, 'What do you want?' He likes an honest answer. He looks into people and sees more to them, like he did with Peter – and gave him a new name. He saw faithfulness in Peter even though others saw weakness.

When we read a gospel story, we can pause here and there and ask, what is new in this story about Jesus? Or what is new about myself?

The gospel is always new. It is a treasure chest to bring out new aspects of the truth of Jesus each time we read it. In prayer he has time for each of us. They stayed with him for a long time and he does not seem to hurry them. The Lord is not in a hurry with us in any way except to love us.

> *Let the words 'come and see' echo in your*
> *mind and heart today and this week.*
> *Lord, thank you for calling me to the Eucharist;*
> *thank you for calling me into prayer.*

3ᴿᴰ SUNDAY IN ORDINARY TIME

The Ordinary

There's something very ordinary for a fisherman about washing nets. Daily work, done with some drudgery but knowing that it is essential for a good catch of fish which would feed the family who, at this time, Jesus called his first apostles.

There is something sacred about the ordinary. About bathing a child, loving a spouse, daily employment, family time and all that makes up our days.

In the middle of all this, God can surprise us and call us into his service. Our expectation is sometimes different – that we need long times of prayer to find God, or read about him, or do *big* things for him. Just as the smallest things are done out of human love, God is found in the ordinary.

The old Irish spirituality had blessings for everything – for milking a cow, cleaning and dusting a room, visiting the sick and many more. There were prayers for meals, for a safe journey and a happy death. Our Irish spirituality found God as much in mountains and people as in the church, and often moreso.

Maybe the disciples remember, in difficult times, the way they were called in their ordinary work, and found their ongoing call to follow the Lord in ordinariness for the rest of their lives.

Give me, O Lord, a love for the ordinary; remind me how ordinary
you were for so much of your life. Amen.

4TH SUNDAY IN ORDINARY TIME

The Power of Evil

Jesus was very aware of the power of evil that can surround us.

Jesus named the spirit. This gave him power over the spirit. He knew evil when he met it and he overcame it with love, power and with kindness.

In Jesus, the good and the evil of the world met.

One big evil in us is selfishness. We learn it from childhood. We take the plate of cakes or a packet of sweets and say 'all mine'. We normally get over this, but not always. We need the conversion from *it's mine* to *it's ours*. That's the Christian way. The environment is not ours, but for us. We have no right to kill off livelihood all over the world for our paper, oil and greed. Any abuse of people is the selfish syndrome. Nobody owns anyone else on this earth and we belong only to God in a free way.

Evil will never win out to the end. It has been conquered on the cross, with love.

Somehow the man in this reading was possessed. Evil came into him and maybe it was not his fault. He left clean and whole, with a kindness in his heart he would never forget. The people were amazed, not just at Jesus, but at the change in the man who had been possessed.

What are the evil desires in myself?
For control of others, for greed, for whatever leads me away from love.
Imagine the light of God filling the darkness in me.
Lead us not into temptation, but deliver us from evil.

5TH SUNDAY IN ORDINARY TIME

Darkness and Light

The first reading is tough to hear and we admire Job. We talk of 'the patience of Job'. Job is the example and the hero of depression. He just had it bad. All had gone wrong and he felt no good, with no hope and no meaning. His family collapsed, his wealth disappeared and he cursed the day he was born. He went through all of the depressions people have, but somehow kept a glimmer of light alive. He never totally lost God, and God never lost him.

Depression is a *huge* illness. Many suffer; many are affected. Treatment can be of help, and the listening times of friends, as well as therapy, is healing.

A great priest once wrote,

At the worst of the burnout I couldn't say Mass, never mind preaching. Dry, empty, without light or life. Thanks again for the card you sent. It means a lot to me now. Funny, in the worst of my anxiety, nothing, no compliment and no reassurance ... meant anything to me.

There are many things that help on a human level. There is the help also of faith and prayer at times; the help of someone who listens, sympathises, reserves judgement and does not offer easy cures (or 'quick fixes'). Love from God never ends, even though it may not appear near just now. This is the Jesus of the gospel – bringing the grace of healing, of freeing from evil, of constant love.

Imagine a time of darkness in life; picture it in its colour, and imagine the bright light of Jesus penetrating that darkness.
Ask for help and give thanks for help. Give light, Good Lord, to all who live in the valley of darkness and the shadow of doubt.

6TH SUNDAY IN ORDINARY TIME

People Make a Difference

Any story involving leprosy is a story of inclusiveness with Jesus. The people whom nobody wanted were deep in his heart. Jesus wanted to make his life better and, in this case, the man was cured. The news spread of this new religious man, a prophet maybe, but one who went where nobody else would go.

Jesus sees into the heart and there he finds a home, because God his Father lives in each of us. His motivation is his deep relationship with all of us. He will cleanse any of the unacceptable sides of ourselves so that we see ourselves as an image of God, forgiven and clean. Can we see others like that?

Who would be the people he would reach in this way today? Maybe the people who want to change their lives from condemnation by self and others. We can name them often, and our society can be cruel on prisoners and their families, abusers of any sort, prostitutes, victims of STIs and many others. He offers a way out of condemnation and that is often through the goodness and care of another. When we come to him we meet his followers, and that also can make a difference.

Recall someone who made a difference in your life at a bad time.
Give thanks!
Jesus, healer of souls, heal what keeps me from loving like you.

7TH SUNDAY IN ORDINARY TIME

Helped by Others' Faith

We would all say that our faith and Christian life has been helped or hindered by other people. The faith of one influences the faith of all, in the family, the community and the neighbourhood.

Faith for the paralysed man opened a door to a living relationship with God in Jesus. Faith was the door opening to the forgiveness of sins, and then to the cure of the sick man. It was the faith of others that brought him to Jesus. We have no evidence that he himself even wanted to go.

The faith of all helped the sick man – he was healed by 'their' faith. Our faithful time of prayer may help people we know or do not know. Our example of faith can influence people in our local circle even though we may be unaware of it.

Many people would like faith to be private. They would prefer it to have no effect or influence on politics, education, health care and many other issues of society. While faith does not wish to impose, it wishes to have some say in the ordinary issues of life.

The man who owned the house in the gospel incident today lost the roof of his house. Sometimes the faith and convictions of others will effect change in our lives. Faith asks for openness to the goodness and the issues of others. Sometimes we will be challenged in the community of faith, perhaps by someone's life, by a homily or by the story of another's faith.

In the best of Christian community, healing and new life happens as it happened for the paralysed man and as it happened for those who brought him to Jesus.

Remember with thanks people who have been
influential in the growth of your faith.
Lord, I believe in your love and care for me. Strengthen my belief.

8TH SUNDAY IN ORDINARY TIME

Good and Bad Religion

Some of those who heard Jesus would have been disciples of John the Baptist. They were constantly challenging Jesus about his difference from John. Jesus praised John very well: 'Nobody better was born of woman', but he knew the message he had was different.

John preached much about the wrath of God and the severity of divine judgment. Fasting and penance were central to his message. He preached repentance for the forgiveness of sin; Jesus preached repentance to believe the Good News.

We don't get the impression that John had good news! We see Jesus eating with sinners, opening his heart to all sorts of outcast people like lepers and prostitutes, and concerned more for the widow and the orphan than for the worship of the temple.

This is the new wine Jesus talks about; this is the new wine of total forgiveness and compassion of God our father. The new skin is the teachings of Jesus and his way of life.

Religion can do good things for people or bad. It can encourage openness to others, especially the poor, or it can drive us in on ourselves. Good religion embraces the best in us all, bad religion continuously points out the worst. Good religion holds on to the best in our neighbour, bad religion to the worst.

The word of Jesus is new each day we read our gospel. It makes us new also, allowing the gospel to point out the goodness of us all.

Remember a time when you had a new insight or belief about Jesus.
What brought that about?
Lord, keep my heart, mind and soul open to your message.

9TH SUNDAY IN ORDINARY TIME

Love or Rule

More this week about the revolutionary side of Jesus; not political or violent, but turning some well-believed religious practices upside down.

The Jewish Sabbath had many rules and rituals, and were observed in their totality. Jesus points out that hunger is more important than a Sabbath rule, and that in the end we are to be masters of the Sabbath, not the Sabbath of us.

This tension goes through all religion. The externals, which were once perhaps connected to the internal and the essential, become all important. We remember the many tiny rules of Roman Catholicism like fasting before communion, collations during Lent and many more.

More serious were rules about marriage and sexuality which have caused great grief for many people. Inter-church rules made some excellent relationships impossible. We can list many frustrations, and they belong mostly, but not exclusively, to the past. We remember the condemnations of people who 'broke the rules'.

The centre of Jesus' message is whether all of our ritual and practice in religion is at the service of love, and particularly at the service of love of the poor.

Love has its practices and laws and rituals; when these are no longer faithful to love, they are no longer faithful to Jesus.

Take a few moments out of doors; feel the wind on your face. This reminds us of the Spirit of God, the environment of love all around us. Lord, may your message always expand our hearts in love of others, especially those who may differ from us in anything religious.

10TH SUNDAY IN ORDINARY TIME

Who is the family of Jesus?

Jesus seems here to disown his family. Does he dismiss Mary and his family? He knew that he was not going down well with the family, and maybe wanted some distance from them. It is interesting that they came for him, maybe to take him home.

But he turns the family table. He expands his notion of the family. Coming from God his Father, he proclaims that all around him are family to him – these are his mother, brother and sister. He will later teach them to pray, not My Father, but Our Father.

This is one of the central teachings of Jesus, that we are all brothers and sisters, because of our Father in heaven. From this truth that Jesus felt so strongly came much of his preaching – to retreat each other as family at its best would.

This follows on from the debate about good and bad religion of earlier weeks. The best of religion treats us all as brothers and sisters because of God. Our first and last belonging is that we belong to God – we come from God and go to God.

There will often be conflict in Jesus' family about him. His first family did not take easily to his new family – his disciples. Only at Pentecost, around the mother of Jesus, would both families unite.

His words are relevant to us today – he looks around at us and sees us as his brothers and sisters. This sentiments makes a difference to how we view each other.

Think of different people and say within yourself,
'You are my brother, you are my sister'.
Make me, Lord, an instrument of peace and of joy among your people.

11ᵀᴴ SUNDAY IN ORDINARY TIME

The Ordinary Jesus

Very often we notice the ordinariness of Jesus. He gives no big discourse on the kingdom of God, he Just looks around him and says it's like seeds growing and you can't see them growing.

People knew what he was talking about – seeds growing down in the ground and you can do little about it! You just wait. They had little of the modern quick ways of sowing, all life was slow and that's often the way.

Like the tiny beginnings of a baby, all through life some of the best things are under our eyes and we do not see them. Coming to death, there is a slow journey often and, like the seeds growting, it is happening under the ground. We are being grown by God always, if only we would let him do it.

How we help others grow, too! You may not know the faith that grows in your children, as faith is different for all of us in practice and specifics; or the way that children are taught to love, love which presents itself in the next generation, where you may see it in a marriage and an ability to forgive and live in peace with each other. Seeds are sown and grow – how to love and forgive, how to share with our neighbour, how to face death. When we remember our dead, what comes to mind is what they taught us about life.

A lot of the best in life comes from waiting. Important moments come at God's time. So much of life is on trust.

Have a look this week at something small that will grow big,
and be amazed!
Heart of God, heart of Jesus, we place our trust in you.

12TH SUNDAY IN ORDINARY TIME

The Sleeping Jesus

In what, for the apostles, was a very bad storm, Jesus slept. It's like he seems asleep in the deep darknesses of life – people's darkness of self-esteem, long-term illness, addiction, migration and all that which causes big storms our lives. But in the friendship and love of God we find we can survive and even grow through them, especially the troubles we have little control over. Even when Jesus was asleep the apostles felt his protective presence.

They found calm only when they were in the middle of the storm. We will find Jesus in the middle of our storms too, when we try not to hide our troubles from him. This was how Job got a bit better in the first reading. His friends were trying to help him avoid his troubles, like take a few drinks or enter a transitory relationship, all the things we do to avoid our troubles. In the middle of the tempest, God spoke to him.

We sit with him in prayer and let him know how we are, and just allow his calm to come over us. We find courage and hope at the Mass and other sacraments, like the great peace of a young man when he received the anointing of the sick, who had left church practice for years. Or the help we can get from the community of people in parish and in the church at bad times. It gives us the courage and strength to deal with the storms in our lives.

Remember a bad time when God seemed to help you. Be grateful.
Protect us from all anxiety as we wait.

13ᵀᴴ SUNDAY IN ORDINARY TIME

Community of Healing

A man had an addictive habit in his life. He said, 'It took me a long time, and countless failures, to realise that you can't change your life simply by willpower. You can only change it by grace and community.' Alcoholics Anonymous has always known this. It's not enough just to have willpower. It's only by touching some higher power, and this is most easily done within a community, that we actually change our lives.

This seems to be in the gospel today. Grace and healing went out from Jesus, and it happened in the community of the disciples and family. A young girl had died at the beginning of her mature life. An older lady had been ill for years. The big ministry of Jesus was for healing and he healed where others did not – among women. People brought people to him, people prayed for each other as we do today, in a community of healing.

The Church needs to rediscover this. Our liturgies can be so individualistic – even how we sit separately, and often 'pray our own thing'. The Mass is our Mass, not mine, not yours. The people at the house of Jairus and the disciples around the woman were together in faith and in prayer. We cannot be Christians on our own. Faith is personal but not private. Our gatherings need more of the communal faith, with a sincere welcome as we enter and a hope to make life better for others as we exit. Ordinary ways too, even a hello on the street, an enquiry about a worry, a helping hand brings the healing love of Jesus as it was brought to the people then.

Become aware of how you need the healing and strength of Jesus, and ask: Lay your hands gently on me, O Lord, and on all who need your healing. Spirit of the living God, heal me and make me whole.

14TH SUNDAY IN ORDINARY TIME

In the Ordinary

It's easy to think you know people, but they can surprise you! We can find ourselves forming opinions and judgements easily about people regarding colour, race or age. Or we know them for a long time and then something happens like a marriage or a death and we see another side to them.

We think the same even about Jesus – was Jesus a carpenter? No! He could work in wood, metal or stone! So immediately we are challenged by this gospel. Here was the ordinary man, going every week to work in Sepphoris, a few kilometres from his home, now taking on the role of preacher and prophet. There's nothing divine about that – or maybe it's one of the most divine things we can do! Work and family bring us close to God, who is working all the time and who is loving all the time.

How might you see God today – creation, love, silence, care? A new baby in the family (i.e. God's creation of new life with us), or someone who is very ill? Remember that weakness of the body can also generate inner peace in the prospect of heaven, and that is God at work. God is around us in the deep moments of life.

What does this gospel make of Jesus? He makes sense of our lives with us and for us, teaching and healing with compassion and love. We do not know him fully, we don't know all he said, but live by the echo of his words.

Think over yesterday – what gave you a lift in the heart,
a sense of peace, the presence of God.
Lord, I thank you for the wonder of us all!

15ᵀᴴ SUNDAY IN ORDINARY TIME

Journey of Faith

There is a certain freedom about accepting the word of God and the gospel of Christ. Jesus tells his disciples not to force the truth of the gospel on people. If they don't accept it and welcome it then they are to move on.

The journey of faith is a long, complicated journey. People accept bits and pieces at times, and remain open to further growth. We sometimes expect too much of people and forget that their life stories and their struggles may make it too much to accept a lot of the gospel. Is the person whose spouse left him or her condemned forever to a single life? Or are some types of criminal people never to be forgiven and welcomed back to the Church?

The reason the apostles would walk away is that people would not listen to them, not that they would not do what they said. We hope for an openness to the gospel from people, as we hope for an openness to everyone's life story when we try to share the word of Jesus.

This is true for parents and teachers; we open the word of God and the truth of Jesus to younger people, and hope that now or later they will be followers of Jesus. It does not happen immediately.

The prophet Amos seems to come from an ordinary job to be a prophet; from the ordinary ways we try to follow Christ, and live out the gospel, we can share the best of our faith with another generation.

Have I judged too easily? Ask for a heart open to the
struggles and history of others.
Lord help me to see others as you see them.

16TH SUNDAY IN ORDINARY TIME

Seeking the Lost

If we see someone who is lost, we naturally want to help them. Those who were lost got Jesus into action, like the shepherd and the lost sheep of the time. Not just a 9–5 and time off; he seemed in some way to know and recognise his own sheep. They had a personal sort of relationship, where every sheep was special. Jesus loved all the sheep, particularly the lost one. He would go looking for them with a heart of love to find them. One by one.

He searched for them with compassion. This is the big word of the kingdom of God. Compassion is received and offered in personal knowledge. Compassion is entering into the world of another, joyful or sad, so that we feel with them. We may not know exactly how others feel, but we can enter into their mood and the tones of their life.

We need to always discover the personal in God and among each other. We live in a very impersonal world if we allow it. Text messages and emails can be very official at times when we may be better served by the tone and emotive forces of our voice. Our heart can go out and that is like the good shepherd; we can be like that good shepherd to others. If you see someone who is lost, do you have a laugh at them? Or are you able to remember a time when you were lost too? Remembering can help us to be compassionate.

The challenge for us in the parish and the church, and every-where, is to reach out to all. That's what Jesus did and that's a big mark of the reign of God on earth.

Recall in prayer who in your family or friendship circle
may be lost in some way. How can you help?
Lord, may your kingdom come.

17TH SUNDAY IN ORDINARY TIME

Open Air Meal

Ordinary bread is a reminder of the Eucharist. Jesus ate among the people; the fragments left over have been our bread ever since. From this gospel mystery, we know we are always worthwhile in God's eyes – everyone is fed equally. We approach the bread of life not because we are saints, but because we need it.

We know also that our offering is valuable: five loaves and two fish of the poorest type, the leftovers on the shelf. The sardines only the poor ate: the boy had no idea of where his offering would lead. We never know where love will bear fruit.

God is with us in the ordinary – the God of the table, not just the temple. Where we are in life, he finds us, and feeds us most when we are most empty. We have often blocked good people from the table of God for too long.

He will feed us always – there is more than enough love in the heart of God for all. The meal of today has lasted, and the Eucharist is the central prayer and activity of the Church. We minister the bread of life now to each other.

At Mass we meet the Lord Jesus, in his death and resurrection – each Mass is our entering into this mystery of prayer and love for the world. This is the active love of God, seen also in our service of his people.

As I eat bread this day, I might remind myself of the two breads –
bread of earth for the body and bread of heaven for the soul.
Lord, thank you for our daily bread.

18TH SUNDAY IN ORDINARY TIME

The 'I' Word

Jesus is a man of the 'I' – but not in a boastful way! He speaks of the bread in the desert, the manna which nourished the people in their wanderings. He builds on their belief in a bread from heaven, but now he himself is the bread. The bread gives life to the soul. He is this bread.

Our Christian faith is centred on a person, not on a book. The gospel is the book of life because it is the book of Jesus. Jesus is our life because he comes from God. So, at times, we call this the bread of heaven.

Is there a more ordinary way for heaven and earth be linked than in the most ordinary of foods? In another country, Jesus might have said that he is the 'rice' of life. It means that in the ordinary events of our lives, God is very near in Jesus. He makes his home in us as the bread we eat becomes part of us.

It is the same story when it comes to love – our faith at all times links human and divine love, and human love of all sorts is a share in the divine life of love. Can we really believe this? That the next time you really love your child, your friend, your spouse or anyone in your life, you are bringing them a piece of God!

That is one of the main reasons why we want to live in love. That we link heaven and earth, divinity and humanity, Jesus and ourselves. Then the 'I' of Jesus becomes the 'we' of his earthly body and presence.

Breathing in and out – let the word 'love' echo in your
mind and heart on the inbreath and the outbreath.
Lord, thy kingdom come!

19TH SUNDAY IN ORDINARY TIME

Food for Now and Eternity

Elijah needed food for both the body and the soul, for forty days which in the Hebrew Testament is a symbolic number for a journey of the soul.

Food for the soul can be, for example, prayer, a good chat at a bad moment or the Mass. Culture, art, music and prayer feed the soul. The bread of life of Jesus is both Holy Communion and other nourishment for the soul.

Pierre Teilhard de Chardin SJ writes, 'We are spiritual beings on a human journey'. This means that at our deepest we are spiritual beings. Our essence is from God and for God, and the journey is human. Both are one.

In amongst all of this is the presence of Jesus. He is our bread of life, and through us he feeds others in many ways. In receiving the bread of life we commit ourselves to being 'Eucharist people' offering the love and compassion of God to the world.

Sometimes we have to wait, and maybe sift through different moods. In the waiting is where the feeding occurs. We are being fed all the time by God, and sometimes we don't notice. The Eucharist is the summit of other feedings and meals.

Our hopes of life after death and our resurrection give the food that always lasts. At the time of death, we need reminders of meeting God in the next life!

We might picture people in great need – of food,
of meaning in life or of hope.
Pray for them, offering to bring food for body and soul when we can.
Give us this day our daily bread, O Lord.

20TH SUNDAY IN ORDINARY TIME

The Best and the Worst

Perhaps you can recall the homely smell of freshly-baked bread – a good beginning to the day. But bread has to be baked under great heat. The wheat is crushed. Both quite brutal. This is a way of saying that in life there is the joy and the pain; and things can go wrong. Life's joys and sorrows are a mixture, and much of the best has some of the worst. The bitterest pain can be when a loved one dies, but you would never cancel out the love for the pain. Death is like that – the worst of life leads to the best of eternity. We often find something great in the worst of times. If we get good exam results, we forget the pain of the work required to achieve them.

The best and the worst in Jesus' life are in the bread and wine of the Mass. The Eucharist recalls the love of God and the cruelty of the human race, all at the one time. Love given and received, but also torture and death at the hands of cruel people.

At the Eucharist, we hold up the world's goodness and joys, along with its depressions and failures, and ask God to be with us in both. Bread symbolises what is good, wine symbolises the pain – this is a way of viewing the Eucharist.

Come and eat, come and offer; the best and the worst. The host we receive is the full and real Jesus, pain and all. It is truly the bread of life and the cup of salvation.

Imagine Jesus offering you some bread:
this ordinary food is the bread of life.
When we eat the bread and drink of the cup,
we proclaim your death, O Lord,
until you come again.

21ST SUNDAY IN ORDINARY TIME

Our Choices

We remember big and small choices in life. Ones that had a significant influence on our lives like a job, marriage, retirement or redundancy; having an operation or many more. Or choices regarding the children that effected their lives – a school change, moving house or perhaps health issues.

Life is made up of many choices, big and small. Human, spiritual and religious choices.

Peter had this sort of choice today. Would he follow Jesus or leave like others did? He stayed but the choice would present itself to him repeatedly. Why did he stay? Our choices are influenced by feelings deep within us; we need Christ within us if we are to follow him.

Peter had enough love for Jesus within him to make this choice. It was not always easy, and he would give in at one point, only to return later. His choice was eventually to answer Jesus' question – do you love me? – positively.

The choice for Jesus is the choice for love, in all sorts of ways, for those near at hand. If you choose Jesus then events large and small – the hunger of the world, as well as the tears of a baby – affect you. What we do in love for others comes from the deepest part of our beings. We need to fill our lives with Christ to be able to share this love in big and small ways.

We need the company of other 'choosers'. The community of faith and of the Church. Peter says, 'to whom shall *we* go?' We follow Christ together.

*Let those words, 'To whom shall I go, Lord?', echo in your prayer
and talk to the Lord about how you feel.
Lord we pray for support and strength in our following of you.*

22ND SUNDAY IN ORDINARY TIME

With Lips or Heart?

When it comes to some vegetables, you eat the leaves and the outside. With an artichoke, the best part is the heart! The best of religion is of the heart. Jesus today talks a lot about that, in contrast to lip service and that are hearts far from him.

The people who were wondering about sincerity kept the law but then were intolerant of weakness in others. They often missed people's goodness and so they gossiped of people who didn't wash their hands, cups and God knows what else.

The heart is the place of *true* religion.

That sentiment is echoed in a variety of everyday phrases too, such as to get to the heart of things; to say that a person has great heart; to put your heart into something; to say that their hearts are miles away.

The heart is a dangerous place. The head will try to be sensible and weigh options against eachother – such as to let the third world look after itself, after all they are spending on war – but the heart will be broken by the hunger of the poorest and moved to action. The head will tell you that you need sleep but your heart will get up to care for a baby or an elderly parent. So the religion of some of Jesus' time was safe – the rules were kept, but was there love?

The heart of religion is found in the heart of God. Kahlil Gibran, in *The Prophet*, writes, 'When you love, do not say "God is in my heart" – say "I am in the heart of God."' This is echoed by St Ignatius when he said, 'Love is seen in deeds not words'.

In prayer allow God touch your hopes to love well in life.
Teach me your truth O Lord, in the sincerity of my heart.

23RD SUNDAY IN ORDINARY TIME

In the Ordinary

Jesus avoids attention after his work of healing the deaf man. He's not a quarter-hour celebrity, he didn't want admiration, he wanted love to flow into and out of ourselves – doing good quietly. The best of things are ordinary. In the ordinary, Jesus worked the miracle and in the ordinary we will hear new things.

The theologian, Karl Rahner SJ, was once asked whether he believed in miracles. His answer was, 'I don't believe in them, I rely on them to get through each day!' Indeed, miracles are always present within our lives, the miracles of birth, of love, of hope. These are the ways that people get over hurts and forgive. Someone giving a lot from the little they have; it is the world of mystery – of little miracles. A miracle is not against nature, it is something that inspires faith and love.

The first reading sees more in the desert than wilderness and flowers: we see and hear beyond created things to the healing work and word of the Creator. Maybe we'll listen to new voices about God and life in our conversations; I recently heard a young person talking about the suicide of a friend and how this brought him to realise how much we really need God. His chat strengthened my faith.

Can we recover the simplicity of life with the small miracles that get us through every day? All of us have something new to say about God and life, and the simplicity of life offers us more than we know.

> *Think today of something small that can remind you*
> *of something deeper and God.*
> *Praise to you, O lord, for simple surprises in my life!*

24TH SUNDAY IN ORDINARY TIME

Losing and Finding

Giving up is part of life – you give up your time and money for your children and grandchildren. You say it was worth it for the joy in their faces. You go to work for the poor, giving up a better job in the process. You want to study more, so you give up some leisure time to do so. In sport people sacrifice a lot to train in order to achieve. But something else comes through for us when we give something up; if it's real and true we receive a lot in return. It seems strange for Jesus to say, 'Lose your life to save it'. He's talking about losing good things in order to get better.

This can be a big challenge in society today, as culture is very centred on the self and care of the ego.

It's rather normal to find that personal concerns take total precedence, without enough care for others. However, it's worth remembering that as long as one person on this globe is hungry, homeless or seeking refuge, the work of Jesus is never done. Losing life and saving life with Jesus is a call to community, to neighbourhood and the world, to make our part of the world a better place.

My own life may be *my* main concern, my circle of care may be drawn firmly around myself, ignoring the sustained care required by the stranger or the outcast. If this is the case, I am called to the challenge of the gospel to relinquish my selfishness and find the generosity in my heart, given by God.

Think ahead to today or later this week. Offer love and service to God.
Lord, teach me to be generous in your service.

25TH SUNDAY IN ORDINARY TIME

The War Inside

There have been many wars in recent years, but James speaks of another battlefield: wars of good and evil and conflicting desires within ourselves. In every war there is evil fighting in the souls of the generals. It's the same with ourselves, good things emerge to be done and we allow other less good motivations to take over. Perhaps we need to visit someone who is sick but there is a match on TV; maybe we offered to help a neighbour, but there's a party on we'd like to go to; visit the parents and something else happens, go to Mass, but the sun starts shining and we go to the beach! Alternative desires, such as to control people, excessive greed or sexual exploitation of the young and not so young, stem more from personal experience. Big-time greed might well have its roots in a fight over an ice-cream at home as a child, or growing up in a household where somebody always got their way at the expense of others.

Jesus' saving love can help us to bring out the best in ourselves. His cross is our peace, within ourselves and within nations. This is the reconciliation that Jesus promises from the cross: peace within us and peace among us.

The apostles got into a row who was the greatest – they wanted to follow Jesus, but something else took over.

Can we bring into ourselves the best of the child that Jesus praises and find God the Father whom we trust? Can we be happy to rest in the regard he has for us, with no need to worry about who is the greatest?

With every inbreath, breathe in God's love and allow it fill your being.
Heart of God, heart of Jesus, I place my trust in you.

26TH SUNDAY IN ORDINARY TIME

Making a Difference

There's a certain definiteness in the gospel today. Like a team taking to the sports field, we are either with Jesus or against him, and this is proven in our way of life. Following Jesus does not necessarily mean being different from others. It means throwing ourselves into the everyday life and needs of people and giving what we can.

In public life we can make our voices heard about issues which deeply effect others, like respecting and protecting life, like ensuring we care for our children in practice as well as in law, like legislating wisely about marriage, how we legislate for the care of our elderly. We may work to free our country from the effects of addiction to drugs and alcohol.

Jesus is asking for a defined lifestyle and a desire to make a difference. Faith is more than assent of the mind, but a way of life and of trust – a way of life that does not hinder others, but rather helps them through compassion and good deeds. Our way of life is a sharing of faith one to another, Pope Francis says that, 'Faith is passed on by contact, from one person to another, just as one candle is lighted from another.'

The people who make a difference are building blocks, not stumbling blocks. Every good cause will inevitably have its begrudgers. The apostles are a good example, and they, bit by bit, realised that following Jesus can be interpreted in many ways. In the giving of cold water or hot soup, or in making a difference to another in any way at all, is being a true follower.

Remember a time you made a difference in someone's life.
Ask to continue to be able to do this.
Lord, teach me to serve you as you deserve.

27TH SUNDAY IN ORDINARY TIME

Reaching Out to Family

The followers of Christ can be caught between valuing the commitment of life's promises in marriage and compassion for people whose marriages have broken up. Jesus values the commitment too: adultery is condemned as a sin against justice – it's seen as tampering in some way with the commitment made by one person to another.

Why is this followed by a comment that children should come to him? My reading is that it is from his love for children, and also for his love of the child inside each of us, the child of God that we all are. So, for the child of God who is suffering through the breakdown of commitment, Jesus is encouraging them to come to him and be welcomed into his arms and blessed.

While trying to value commitment in marriage, and also in religious life, he is reaching out to people who are in difficult personal situations. We follow him in this, letting go of judgements about people's relationships.

The Church has tried in many ways to reach out to people who need care, protection and healing in Pope Francis's letter on the family, *The Joy of Love*.

In situations where there are differences in people's attitudes, especially in the family, it is good to keep avenues of communication open. This is the way towards greater love and healing, and allowing Jesus to be part of every aspect of life. Many parents have been happy in later years that they kept lines of communication open with children whose lifestyles may have been different from theirs.

Think of a family relationship for which you are grateful.
Lord, may your love be upon us, especially in our commitments.

28TH SUNDAY IN ORDINARY TIME

Real Riches

The preacher had placed a mirror at the end of the church. He asked everyone to look into it and at the edge of the mirror was written, 'This is your greatest treasure'. The rich man in the gospel thought treasure was in wealth, and this made him sad. The wisdom of Jesus is that wealth is not the final happiness. Our biggest treasure is inside ourselves: each of us made in the image of God, by love and for love.

Does our culture today value the dignity of each person and the treasure that each person is? It's good to have a nice house, but a shame that it uses so much energy and generates such expense. Do our hospitals, who care for the elderly and many others, value the dignity and the treasure that each person is? Can we go into A&E and say that all these people are treasures, or are they just trolley-holders?

God's best gift to any parish is its people. Like in a school, or any institution which gathers people together. The rush of life and a general societal self-centredness can take the focus off the essential aspects of communities and people. The gospel today asks us to look to the right place for our true wealth and riches – to our charity, to our giving of time and self to others in the sort of relationships of love which value the worth and dignity of all.

I picture people I know and give thanks to God for each of them.
Let your face shine on us, O Lord,
that we may see your reflection in each other.

29TH SUNDAY IN ORDINARY TIME
Servant of All

The gospel this week is a story of ambition cloaked in good intentions. A mother wants her sons in the best place, and they pick up that ambition from her. The apostles see James and John as wanting to be close to Jesus. Jesus accepts this, but lets them know that to be close to him means to suffer with him, and to be a servant.

We see this many times in the gospel: giving a cup of cold water was a servant's job, washing the guests' feet was a servant's job. Jesus brought service even further in undertaking these tasks himself. To serve like him was to serve god his Father, because that was his mission on earth.

We hear often of the servant Church – it means that the community of Jesus' followers are at the service of people, aiming to improve people's quality of life, to live and share with compassion in the hardships of others, to care for the earth and protect it. This service of people is the service of God. In that mission Jesus would be misunderstood, and eventually put to death.

Even after death we see him as a sort of servant of the apostles – reaching out to them to share his joy and consolation. He would be the one to walk with them in their doubts, fears and disappointments. It would appear that he is a servant in his risen life too.

Think of the day ahead or the week,
and offer yourself in the service of the Lord.
Lord may I serve you and be with you in all I do and care for.

30TH SUNDAY IN ORDINARY TIME

All That He Needed

When we feel compassion, we are reaching out to others. Someone's tears get us crying, or their joy gets us laughing. Compassion reaches into the needs of another, and simply wants to be there and to help.

Our gospel today is a response to an illness. The story of a blind man who shouted at Jesus to hear him – there was no whispered or shy prayer here! His faith made him shout to Jesus and believe that he could be healed. He threw away what precious little he had – a cloak – and knew he had found all he needed, the faith that made him strong. His faith gave him energy as he jumped at the sound of Jesus' name.

Although his sight returned, this was not until later; the first gift was faith. Our faith helps us to see the world as God sees it. We see creation as the beauty of God and care for it, we see other people as images of God and we care for them. We see beyond labels and categories to everyone as a child of God, and as our brothers and sisters. This is the 'eye of faith'.

The way of Jesus is the way of light, and of healing, so that nothing within ourselves can block us from receiving the light of God, the light of his love.

Imagine the dawn gradually bringing light to the darkness.
Does this remind you of what light of God you might pray for?
Lighten our burdens lord, enlighten our darkness
and may we walk in your ways.

31ST SUNDAY IN ORDINARY TIME

What is Religious?

We often ask people what is most important to them in life. Various themes come to mind: family, faith, love, peace of mind, money – the list is infinitely varied. Jesus is asked something like this in the conversation of today's gospel. His most important word is love – anything in the religious tradition of the time is secondary to love of God and love of the neighbour.

In August 2012 a survey indicated that the Irish are among the least religious people of Europe. This sample size of 1,000 people and indicates something to do with religious understanding and practice. It would, however, not be an unreasonable challenge to say that we are amongst the *most* religious, not necessarily when we are in church or praying, but when we are at our most loving and caring, or concerned for justice.

True religion is just that, it shows particularly when people care for the needy. Jesus' heart went out mostly to the needy in his own time, especially any group who were outcast, such as those suffering from leprosy.

The same can be true of us today. Jesus is the one on the side of the needy, and the one who is most on our side when we are in need. This is the meaning and the reason for the Christian community – to be bearers of love in our world. We should bear love to those in our world who are in the greatest need, just as Jesus did.

So maybe in Ireland we are much more religious than the survey shows! When we love, then we are religious in the name of Jesus.

Recall moments when you thought you were most 'religious';
Lord, may I find your love and call in everything I encounter this day.

32ND SUNDAY IN ORDINARY TIME

A Series of Contrasts

The gospel is a series of contrasts – rich and poor, greedy and generous, arrogant and humble – and it is not difficult to guess which of them Jesus is praising. The lady in question, a poor widow, may not even have heard the praise of Jesus but the disciples were left in no doubt where his sympathies lay.

He praises true religion in the widow, who gave all she had in the cause of God. He berates the co-existence of long prayers and the greed which took away the property of people like this widow. The religious people of the day were meant to look after the widow and the orphan, who had nobody else to fight their cause.

From the gospel we take the invitation of Jesus to give all; the amount given is not the big question, it is the giving of the heart. Jesus knows the listeners would understand that what he was talking about was more than money – it was to give the first place in life to God and that which came from God. That is the call to all of us.

That which came from God is the love we are called to receive and to give, the love which inspires us to care for other things of God like creation, justice, peace and reconciliation. It is to give time to worship God in common and in private – to ensure a space and time for prayer in each day.

The widow of the gospel had a generous heart, as did the widow in the first reading. They looked outward to the needs of others and the things of god, and gave what they could in this direction. Can we not do the same?

'Lord teach me to know you more, love you more and serve you more faithfully in my life' – St Ignatius Loyola

13:24-32

33RD SUNDAY IN ORDINARY TIME

Reminder from the Tree

The tree was an important image for Jesus – he spoke many truths of his message pointing to trees, like mustard seeds which grew big, vines that withered, and the fig tree which was common to his hearers. When asked about the signs of things to come, he gave no long homily, but instead looked at a fig tree and said you know from this when summer and winter is coming. In the same way, we can sense his presence in our lives in different ways. This may not help us to know about the end of time and the questions people had then, but it can get us to become aware of how God is present in our lives.

The word of God is spoken in the human words of many people. In kindly, forgiving and tolerant words, and also in the word of God spoken in the Mass, Jesus speaks to us today. Like the people looking at the fig tree, we can find his presence in the kindliness and helpful words of another. This is the word of God in human form. It will not pass away.

We are called to speak his word in our way of life: to be friends of the earth, friends of all people, including the poor. That's redemption, Jesus and ourselves working in unison.

God's book of compassion and love includes our names. We can be thankful that our names are in the book of life.

Imagine a blank page of the book of life: see your name on the page,
and a list of the good you have done.
Lord bring more good out of what I have tried to do
in my life out of love.

FEAST OF CHRIST THE KING

What type of King?

An important part of life is where you come from, and we are often judged for it. Sometimes we judge *totally* based on where people are from, as Pilate with Jesus. With all he knew had heard of him – the miracles and the speeches – we still heard, *'Where are you from? Are you a king really? What sort is your kingdom?'*

Pilate was intrigued with Jesus and so are we.

Our Christian life is about getting to know Jesus more, taking part in his mission, becoming the type of person he was; knowing that he came from God and from humanity. He speaks of the best of God and the best of us, the best of heaven and the best of earth. He is worthy of our following.

Our role in life, our vocation and our mission is a calling to live like him in love and service.

There is an aspect of 'from above' regarding Jesus, and much of John's Gospel stresses the divinity of Christ. He doesn't look very divine, but he does look very human. In the human is the divine. So we could be like him. We become like him by reading about his life and living like he did. He is a king in his truth, justice, compassion and love. The king-defender of the poor.

This is a good ending of one Church year to begin another – king and servant. We'll see more of what it's all like in the weeks of December. In the meantime, we want to live in this reign of God and pray and live – *your kingdom come.*

> *Picture Jesus with Pilate, mocked and belittled.*
> *Or on the cross, and recall, 'This man is a king'.*
> *Jesus, remember me, when you come into your kingdom.*

MISSION SUNDAY

Become bearers of the Good News of Christ (Pope Francis)

Many are 'missionaries' at home, as parents, family members and in ordinary love and friendship. Others are 'missionaries' in the form of parish ministers, chaplains in schools, hospitals and prisons, some as priests and religious, others as lay people. All are called with the pouring of baptismal water to be missionaries for Christ. Mission Sunday is the day we recall that we are all people on a mission, sent by the Risen Lord to share in his love for the Father, and to share this love with others.

Today we remember in a special way our people – priests, religious and lay - who have gone abroad to work in countries much less prosperous than our own. Countries which lack schools, hospitals and other necessities we take for granted; countries which possess displaced people, people who are being trafficked, those who are modern slaves and others who are suffering immensely. They are answering a call to be men and women of Jesus Christ, in service of others.

They appreciate our prayers, our texts, calls and many other communications to them; they are dependent often on our financial contributions to keep their work going.

Today is a day to remind ourselves of their good work, and the improvement in quality of life that they drive in developing countries. May we never lose our goal to spread the love of God, and be mindful that the people of the developing world give us joy in life and faith, that brings us in touch with the joy of giving a lot even when people have little. Their mission is our mission.

Recall people you know who are missionaries today and pray for them.
Send forth your Spirit, O Lord, and renew the face of the earth.

DECEMBER 8ᵀᴴ, IMMACULATE CONCEPTION OF MARY

Mary – Strong and Fragile

Mary seems to find God in the ordinary human side of her life and in her fragility. A bit like John the Baptiser, who is another advent figure – no pomp or ceremony is present. He was a man clothed in fragility and poverty.

Since Mary knew weakness, she could know God. She could shout to all that, 'God does great things for me'. If we think we have things all together, then we find little need for God. God will be missing, and not missed.

Much of the gospel of her Son will be finding and helping people at their worst. She will often be present at times of people's great needs, like at the wedding feast of Cana and later at Calvary. Jesus seems drawn to these sort of people.

It's the same for ourselves. We are loved most by God when we are at our weakest.

The Church is currently at a weak and fragile moment in time. Scandals of sex abuse have weakened us; the pride and pomposity of the institution has often dulled the word of God. The Church is no longer as influential as before. We need prayer and the example of Mary to rediscover Jesus in our community. Jesus is our inspiration as God cares for us in our lowliness.

Like Mary, turn to him for life and strength and the courage to live his gospel and believe his promises.

What aspect of Mary helps you in your Christian life? Give thanks!
Holy Mary, mother of God, mother of the Church, pray for us always.

MATTHEW 2:1–12

JANUARY 6TH EPIPHANY

Changing Paths

We may think that they got to the end of their journey when they got to Bethlehem. The star led them there, and the star rested, like themselves, after the journey.

What happened there we don't know. They offered gifts and got something in return. Some mood and commitment to the journey home. But the journey would not end. They would still be searching; the journey to the child did not end with the child's birth.

It's the same with ourselves. The journey doesn't end with graduation, marriage, retirement or with any other decisive time in life. The journey of life, and with God, is always developing. The star leads us to God who loves the world and sends us into the world, with protection from danger as the magi found.

To live is to change often. Faith is similar. The magi went back different – they had a different route home and a different map of life inside themselves. Maybe the Epiphany is feast of the changing ways of faith and keeping faith ourselves! The grace of the feast is of the ever-new God, as we are open to new understandings and levels of friendship with him. It's the feast of those who search and who long for God. He would be found in the simplest of places – the ordinary life of the family.

Recall moments when God seemed close, maybe different from before.
Mary, lead us to your Son, lead us to life,
now and in all the hours of life. Amen.

MARCH 17TH ST PATRICK'S DAY

Patrick made a Difference

Tradition portrays him as a slave brought to Ireland from either Wales or France, and left minding sheep on Slemish Mountain, Antrim. We are told that he often prayed all night. He is a reminder of the goodness and faith of young people.

We sometimes think that working for God is only for our adult years, but following Christ is an invitation at all times of our lives.

Young people bring a certain freshness and honesty to our faith. Pope Francis encourages them, 'With [Jesus] we can do great things; he will give us the joy of being his disciples, his witnesses. Commit yourselves to great ideals, to the most important things.'

Regarding youth, he reminds the adults that, 'I like to speak with the youth, and I like to hear the youth. They always put me in difficulty. They tell me things that I haven't thought of, or that I've only partly thought of. The restless youth, the creative youth, I like them!' They may often refresh the faith of the older generation.

We want to share the best of our Christian faith with our young people. For that we need to listen a lot to their questions and hopes. Maybe that's what happened to Patrick later when he escaped from slavery. At a young age he had heard a call, and later he said his 'yes' –Ireland was never the same again!

Patrick frequently prayed at night. End your day with a night prayer of thanks or trust in God.

St Patrick, pray for us, pray for continued peace in our land,
pray for our young people.

AUGUST 15TH
ASSUMPTION OF MARY

A Feast of Hope

It can often be said of someone that they're 'always on about something'; or that they 'never let something go'! Mary was like that. She was always on about hope. She says little in the gospels, but her words were always hopeful. In the middle of the visitation to Elizabeth she sang the *Magnificat*, a song of hope and praise; this is the gospel mostly read at her feast days. She remained in silent hope at the Cross and was a central person to the apostles after the resurrection of Jesus.

That is the meaning of today's feast – Mary's message of hope reaches beyond this life to the next. While she is always on our side – and especially of those in need – she is on our side from the other side. Nothing can take away the hope she shares, for she shared it from eternity.

We need this – now and at the hour of our death. Our world needs this hope – the confidence in faith that God is always with us, always cares and always walks with us in life.

Pope Francis prays on this feast, 'May we not be robbed of hope, because this strength is a grace, a gift from God which carries us forward with our eyes fixed on heaven. And Mary is always there, near those communities, our brothers and sisters, she accompanies them, suffers with them, and sings the *Magnificat* of hope with them.'

> *Look ahead to this day and tomorrow and offer*
> *the good you want to do to God with Mary.*
> *My soul glorifies the Lord, always and everywhere.*

NOVEMBER 1ST, ALL SAINTS DAY

Saints Known and Unknown

In remembering the saints, we remember and honour our heroes of faith, martyrs, known and unknown, leaders of churches who pioneered social reform. We recall the sisters who pioneered medical and educational work. The parents and grandparents, aunts and uncles and other family members and friends who passed on the faith. The priests and religious of parishes throughout the country and around the world in many localities, often in extreme poverty and social difficulties.

Today we also salute the tireless workers for peace and justice throughout the world and in our country. People whose lives have been at risk in their work here and elsewhere in the pursuit of peace. Our saints encourage us to be people of peace, tolerance and inclusiveness in our neighbourhoods.

Our unknown saints remind us that it is possible to live by the vision of the gospel. Maybe every church should have an altar to the unknown saints, like cities have their monument to the unknown soldier which reminds us of all who fought in wars. Our altar would remind us of all who lived lives of faithfulness to God and who handed on faith to a new generation.

I have met a few people over the years that I would call saints. They had much in common in prayer and love, and also in sense of humour. With them there was always laughter – a good sign of holiness!

I recall people in my life who I think were really holy,
and recall what they handed on to me.
For our saints, known and unknown we thank you, O God.
May we join them one day with you. Amen.

MARTIN HOGAN

Weekday Reflections
for Liturgical Year 2017/2018

Let the Word of Christ Dwell in You

€14.95

WWW.MESSENGER.IE
PHONE: 353 1 7758522

The Prayer Book 2018

SACRED
SPACE

THE IRISH JESUITS ✱ Sacred Space
from the website www.sacredspace.ie

€12.95

WWW.MESSENGER.IE
PHONE: 353 1 7758522